CONTENTS

Table Of Contents	3
Introduction	5
What Is A PhD?	7
Structure	10
PhD Team	13
Communicating With Your Supervisors	15
Publications	17
Types of Publications	19
Literature review	37
The Question	43
"Big" Enough	45
Resources	47
Thesis	49
Writing A Journal Paper	50
Introduction	55
Method	59
Results	61
Discussion	67
Conclusion	69
Abstract	71
References	73

Author Order	77
Reviewing And Submitting The Paper	79
How To Respond To Peer-Review Comments	81
How to Write A Conference Paper	86
Preparing And Giving A Conference Presentation	89
Time To completion	92
Personal Citations	93
Zero-Sum Game	96
Learning About Fringe Areas	98
Ergonomics	100
Final Words	102
Other Books By The Author	103

TABLE OF CONTENTS

Introduction

What Is A PhD?

Structure

PhD Team

Communicating With Your Supervisors

Publications

    Types of Publications

    Journal Publications

    Know How Good A Journal Is

    Impact Factor

    Time-To-Publication

    Acceptance Rate

    Blind, Double-Blind

Literature Review

The Question

    "Big" Enough

    Resources

    Thesis

Writing A Journal Paper

    Introduction

> Method
>
> Results
>
> Structuring The Results Section
>
> How To Actually Write The Results Section
>
> Discussion
>
> Conclusion
>
> Abstract
>
> References
>
> Author Order
>
> Reviewing And Submitting The Paper
>
> How To Respond To Peer-Review Comments

How To Write A Conference Paper

Preparing And Giving A Conference Presentation

Time To Completion

Personal Citations

Zero-Sum Game

Learning About Fringe Areas

Ergonomics

Final Words

INTRODUCTION

So, you've made it into your doctoral program. Congrats! It's a big achievement. You managed to get through the interview process and secured your spot. The next few years are going to be full of new experiences and it's important for you to get up to speed with your new surroundings and student path.

Entering Academia is daunting for many students. It's a whole world that you might be unfamiliar with. Terms like "journal article", "double-blind peer review", "research campaign", "literature review", and "citations" are thrown around on a daily basis, and you might be left there with your head spinning from all the new information. What's more, these Academic items play large roles in your PhD, so, they're hugely important.

I remember when I first stepped into Academia to do my PhD all those years ago, and I see the same reaction on my new students' faces every year – this glazed-over look washes over your face, and you're left thinking, "What are all of these things? Are the even speaking English anymore??" The look is somewhat comical to see.

This book goes through the different technical aspects of Academia, and your PhD. It goes through:

- How your PhD differs from the other degrees you've completed

- How to get a jump start
- What publications are
- **How to do a literature review**
- **How to write a journal paper**
- **How to respond to reviewer comments and get your papers accepted!**
- **How to present at a conference**
- and more…

After reading this book, you'll be up to speed with the academic technical items pertaining to your PhD and Academia itself. What's more, you'll be able to understand all those academic conversations that go on in your department.

Let's begin!

WHAT IS A PHD?

A PhD is a process whereby someone of a particular skillset is taken and trained to be able to conduct effective and efficient research in a given field. At its crux, it's as simple as that.

At the start of your PhD, you only need to have the skillset required by entering students. By the end of the PhD, you should have developed the skills of a researcher.

The PhD focuses on a particular "question" – that question is what your PhD is aimed at answering. For example, the question might be something along the lines of, "What is the effect of temperature on Li-Ion battery charging times", or "What is the effect of inflation on small business growth". The question needs to meet the following requirements in order for it to be worth investigating:

1) Important to the funder
2) Well-, and precisely, defined
3) Relevant to your field

The first requirement is perhaps the most important of all; the research you put out should benefit the funder in some way. What that benefit is, is usually determined by the funding body. For example, the funding body might be the environmental agency, and they might want to understand how water vapor affects the "glasshouse effect". So, your PhD research should provide information about that kind of phenomenon. Another example could be a pharmaceutical company, which is looking at a new kind of drug. If the research you plan on conducting doesn't benefit the funder, then that will impact the future grants to your research group – it might even affect your funding during your PhD, as you will probably have some kind of annual review. It might seem daunting, but your supervisors are there to guide the direction your PhD takes, so you shouldn't be left to your own devices.

Catering your PhD research to the funding body's field might seem very difficult, but with practice, it is quite easy. Some questions that you have to ask yourself are:

1) What does the funding body do?
2) What direction is the funding body going?

By answering these questions, you'll get a much better idea of whether the research you are doing will be beneficial for them or not – align your research with the answers to these questions and everyone will be happy. What's more, your project will already have a general direction defined before you start, and so you'll already be fairly dialed-in to what the funder wants. It's just a matter of tweaking that direction to really hone-in on a particular goal and making sure that it still fits what the funder is after.

The second requirement is also important. The more defined your question is, the more impactful your research will be – if you conduct a few experiments or simulations, and they all aim at slightly different questions, then it will be difficult to show how your research is applicable – a little here and a little there means that the data you collect are in all different areas, but they don't really work together to give you a cohesive body of work. By having a well-defined question, your work becomes greater than the sum of its parts; each set of data you collect joins the rest of the data you have, to provide even more insight into a particular phenomenon. Furthermore, the more you work on a particular question, the more knowledgeable you become about it, so every subsequent experiment or simulation will be better, it will be more effective and efficient. On the other hand, if you have a broadly defined question, then you can't really answer it, as it requires a lot more work to give conclusive answers – your work will be a little more superficial, as you spread yourself too thin. By keeping the question pinpoint accurate, you reduce the amount of work you need to do, and increase the applicability of the work you do.

The third requirement is also important as if your question is different to your field, then you might not have access to the knowledge you need to successfully answer it – no one in your research group can help you either. Questions that are partly relevant to your field, but also relevant to other fields are grouped into the "multi-disciplinary" category. It means exactly what it sounds like – it contains aspects from more than one field. These projects are very useful as having greater connectivity among fields increases innovation – you'd be surprised how often something from another field (sometimes, completely unrelated) can help another field. For example, some fields are very mature in error analysis (determining what the error is in your measurements), while other fields don't even consider errors yet. Multi-disciplinary projects can be thought of "cultural-exchanges" – you learn from each other, and the entire project becomes better as a result. What's more, these days, many applications involve more than one field, for example, marketing is greatly helped by machine learning. So, involving more than one field in a project usually makes the project better.

STRUCTURE

A PhD is different to a Bachelor's or Master's degree. Many students who enter the PhD-world bring with them the same general approach that they had in those previous degree – I did too, so you're in good company. It sometimes takes a few months to snap out of that approach and realize that you have to adopt a different approach, and that's okay.

The problem with the approach that most undergrad and Master's students have is that it is well suited to a highly structured program (like a Bachelor's or a Master's degree). In Bachelor's and Master's degrees, things are quite structured – you know that you've got to go to this lecture, or that lecture. You might have a 6-month research project somewhere in there. And once you've done all of that, you'll finish your degree.

In a PhD, things are a little different. Yes, you'll likely have courses to take at some point during the process. And yes, you need to pass them. But the major difference comes in the project phase (the research phase). Depending on which school you attend, the project phase could run for anywhere between 2 years and 6 years (unfortunately, many Universities have longer-than-ideal timeframes). During that time, you work with your supervisors and conduct research. However, this period is very different to the projects you completed in your Bachelor's or Master's degree. In those degrees, the research phase was just a small portion of the overall degree. In your PhD, this research phase is a very large portion. In fact, it is arguably the largest and most important.

Because the research portion of your doctorate degree takes years to complete, the question is usually bigger. The project is often less structured to what you might be used to, and you'll find that a structure needs to be developed. That's where diligence enters. By being diligent in your work, and treating your PhD as a "job", you give yourself the best possible chance of producing meaningful research.

Treating your research as a job is not just about making sure that you work a given number of hours per week, although you definitely should ensure that you keep a working schedule – it increases productivity. It also means that you need to keep track of what deliverables there are, and when they're due. For example, when I was a PhD student, I had to juggle several different tasks all the time. From teaching, to grading, to conducting research, to learning more about my field, to analyzing data, to writing papers, to managing Bachelor's and Master's projects, etc. All of them required me to treat my PhD as a job – I had to take responsibility for delivering them, and delivering them to a high standard. Of course, my supervisors had their input, and they were responsible for many of those items as well, sometimes, even more. But at the end of the day, if I didn't put in the work that I should've, then those items wouldn't get finished.

Another example of how you need to treat your PhD as a job is, last month, one of my PhD students had a conference paper due. The conference is the biggest of the year, and attracts thousands of presenters. In order to get accepted into this conference, his work needed to be top-notch. So, the planning for this paper started almost a year ago – planning what to investigate for the paper, what to include, what not to include, how to write the paper, and when all of these tasks should be completed by. He had his courses, as well as other work to do all the while, so in order to make sure that he would meet the final submission deadline, he had to make a plan and adhere to it. It required organizational skills and treating his work as a job.

A great tool to use is the Gantt chart (or any other type of timeline-tool), where you take note of when things are due and the steps along the way. One of the most important reasons why developing Gantt charts for your PhD is that, it helps you juggle all of the things you need to do. It doesn't matter if you're the only person who even knows about it, it will help dramatically – if another task pops up, then it becomes easy to determine if you can fit it into your schedule. By being more organized and structured in your work, you become more robust to unforeseen problems.

PHD TEAM

When you start your PhD, you join a "team". The team consists of you and your supervisors. This team is focused on your project and you getting your PhD. Your team might fit into a larger team, like a "research group" for example, but your most immediate team is centered around your project. I should note that, like all teams, some work better together than others, and some teams consist of members who have the exact same goals, while other teams don't.

About research groups; your supervisors probably have other students. What's more, they might have other researchers as well, like postdoctoral researchers (people who have finished their PhDs and are doing more research afterwards. These people might be researching the exact same topic as they were during their PhDs, or they might be researching another). All of this research feeds into your supervisors' overall research, and as such, you can think of all of these people as being part of an overall research group. Some supervisors might even have setup a group and called it "The 'Something' research group" – 'something' being the name of the supervisors' research.

In your own team (the team that's focused on your PhD), each member has a particular function. The supervisors are there to provide you with direction, experience, expertise, and advice. If you have more than one supervisor, then it's probably because your project could benefit from the skills and knowledge that each of your supervisors have – the principal supervisor might think that he/she doesn't have all the expertise to be able to run your project efficiently, so he/she invites another academic to join the project and in exchange this new academic becomes another supervisor and gives you support.

Your role in your PhD is to do the work and get trained in your field so that you can conduct effective research later on. So, you effectively take direction from your supervisors, work in that direction, and learn along the way. It's also important to understand what each of the team members wants out of the project.

One final item to note is that, you're the student, so don't ever feel like you can't ask a question – you're there to learn, so if you need clarification on something, or don't understand, then make sure you ask.

COMMUNICATING WITH YOUR SUPERVISORS

Your supervisors are there to help you conduct your research. It might be a little intimidating interacting with them for the first few times, but there's nothing to worry about. They understand that you're new to the process, and that there'll be a learning curve – think about it, you're there to learn. If you knew what you needed to know already, then why would you be there?

Treat your PhD as a learning experience, especially when you first start out. If you don't know something, then you're free to say so.

That leads us onto the next point, keeping in touch with your supervisors.

It is very common for students and supervisors to lose touch. Sometimes, they can go months without ever interacting. That's not a great strategy. You need input, especially when you're starting out. During your first week, your head might be spinning from all the new information – what you think needs to be done in your project will change drastically by the hour. Give it a few more weeks, and your thoughts and opinions will still change, but it might take a few days instead of hour by hour. The thing with all of that information is, if you don't have someone to talk about it with, then you sometimes lose your sense of direction. What's more, if you talk with your supervisors, they can help you determine whether you should start reading about a certain topic or not. What's more, you might actually come up with a great idea that no one (including your supervisors) has thought of – I remember that I had a great idea within the first 4 weeks of my PhD – that idea subsequently created a whole new field a couple of years later, so don't feel like you're ideas aren't as important as anyone else's, you'd be surprised at how profound your ideas can be at times, even when you've just started out in your PhD.

Particularly in the early stages of your PhD, you need to keep a line of constant communication open with your supervisors. Your supervisors have been thinking about your project for a while now, and coupling that with their experience in researching means that they can give you valuable input.

If, at any stage in your PhD, especially when you're first starting out, you lose touch with your supervisors for more than 2 weeks, then you better send them an email to just check in, give them a brief update of what you're doing, and ask them if there's anything else that you should be doing. At the end of the day, the successful completion of your project is not just your responsibility – it's also your supervisors', so make sure to get help from them when you need it.

PUBLICATIONS

Publications are the lifeblood of any research project. Everyone in Academia craves them. Your supervisors desperately want them. Your University desperately wants them. You'll desperately want them, because without them, you won't be able to finish (most PhD programs have a requirement whereby the PhD student needs a certain number of publications in order to finish). I'm going to cover publications in general in this section. I discuss this topic before getting into the "Literature Review" as it's good to have an understanding as to what publications are and how they become publications – it helps you understand which publications should be reviewed in your Literature Review and which ones shouldn't. After this chapter, I'll cover the Literature Review in detail. So, let's continue with discussing publications!

When I first started my PhD, I had next-to-zero knowledge of what a publication was. I wasn't aware of the whole industry built around them. I wasn't aware of the different types of publications, and the relative importance of one. I didn't understand what an "H-Index" was, or the "Impact Factor" of a journal was, let alone what a journal was! So, what are all of these metrics?? What are publications?

TYPES OF PUBLICATIONS

There are two main types of publications: journal and conference. Journal publications are more highly regarded than conference publications. A journal publication (also known as: journal paper, journal article, or just "paper" or "article") is a document that details your research.

Journal Publication

Once you've conducted your research, you need to document it somehow – this is incredibly important, as it is a useful way of passing on the knowledge from one person to the next – you can literally read a publication from 100 years ago and get the information that those researchers found. The publication approach is a highly beneficial one.

One of the most common ways of publishing your findings is the "journal article". Do you remember high school science? Where you did an experiment, then you made a report that consisted of: the introduction, the method, the results, the discussion, and the conclusion. You then handed up that document to the teacher, who graded it and gave it back to you. Journal articles are the same! Like those high school reports, a journal article contains those exact same elements. In addition, you usually have two more elements – the abstract, and the references. The abstract is a summary of the research – it is usually only 200 words or so. The references are a list of other publications that impacted your research.

Journal articles are published in a journal. That means that, other people around the world can download your article and read it – that's how you build your reputation as an academic. We'll get into how to write a journal article later on in the "Writing A Journal Paper" section.

Once you've written the article and your PhD team (you and your supervisors) are happy with it, you send it to a journal; you go online and visit the particular journal's website and you submit it to the journal. During the submission stage, you often need to pick which "editor" to send it to, and list some people whom you'd like to "peer review" your publication.

There are quite a few new items in that last paragraph, so let's break them down.

Editor: The editor is someone who represents that particular journal. An editor is someone who receives paper submissions, initially checks to see whether these papers of a high-enough standard for the journal, and whether they fit the field of the journal. If both of those criteria are met, then he/she sends around some emails to people around the world trying to get them to agree to review the paper. I've received many of these requests, the email typically gives you the abstract and the title, then asks if you'd be happy to review the paper and provide feedback. Once the editor has received acceptance from someone, he/she then sends the paper through for them to review.

Peer Reviewing: Peer reviewing refers to a process where (you guessed it), your peers review your paper. In other words, other people receive your paper and they go through it and give their opinions about it. For a journal paper, you'll usually get anywhere between 2 and 4 reviewers (any less is not good, and any more is highly unlikely due to the difficult nature of getting people to agree to being reviewers). The reviewers' opinions can be about anything in the paper, from the technical content (they might have an issue with an equation that you used), to the figures (maybe the text is too small), to the method (maybe they think that there's a weakness in the method), to not including certain references (Academia is highly competitive, and egotistical, and no academic likes to have their work ignored, so if you do ignore someone's work, then you'll probably hear about it). Now, in the ideal world, the peers reviewing your work would be people who know about your field. In reality, this is not always the case. You might often get people who are on the fringes of your field, or sometimes people who don't know much about it at all. You can tell how much a reviewer knows about your work by what they fixate on. If a reviewer knows a lot about your field, then they'll often ask highly technical questions (for example, about the math involved, or the limitations of the method). The less a reviewer knows about your field, then the less likely they'll be to ask highly technical questions – they'll often just stick to the structure of the paper (for example, "I think that lines 255-265 should be included in the discussion and not the results", or something like that). However, every now and then, you'll get a reviewer who doesn't know much about your field asking highly technical questions – it's usually easy to see that they don't know the field because the questions are almost nonsensical.

Also, sometimes you'll get a rival researcher reviewing your paper. Some of these rivals are nice about it and fair, but others do everything they can to try to stop your paper getting accepted – it's bad for their career and reputation if you get your paper published because then they've got more competition – it's just the nature of the beast.

Once your paper has been sent off for peer reviewing, you usually have to wait a while before you get the comments back – during this time, the reviewers review the paper, give comments back to the editor, the editor makes a decision about what to do with the paper, and then you finally receive all of this feedback.

The editor has a few choices to choose from. His/her choice is usually very influenced by what the reviewers have to say about the paper. The choices are as follows:

1) Accept the paper without revision
2) Accept the paper with revision
3) Revise the paper
4) Reject the paper

The first option, "Accept the paper without revision", is very uncommon – the higher up you go in your field, then the more likely you are of getting this outcome. I remember when I was doing my PhD, I saw this one paper from the top person in my field, that paper was submitted and outright accepted – I hadn't seen another paper like that.

The second option, "Accept the paper with revision", is a fairly common occurrence. This outcome is effectively saying, "The paper is good, but there are a few minor points to work out before we can accept it." If you get this response from the editor, then you should be very happy – it means that your paper is almost accepted, and there's usually only a few minor points to revise.

The third option, "Revise the paper", is not great, but not terrible – your paper was not accepted, but it wasn't rejected. So, you and your supervisors need to figure out whether it's worth putting the effort into revising the manuscript ("manuscript" is a term often used for a paper that hasn't been accepted yet), or if you should just withdraw it and submit it to another journal.

The fourth option is not very pleasant – no one likes having their work rejected. However, I should stress that, having your work rejected doesn't mean that it's of poor quality. I have seen, and been part of, many papers that faced rejections only to become highly cited. In fact, my first journal paper I ever wrote was knocked back by more journals than I can remember, and now it is one of my most cited papers, and one of the leading papers in its field. What's more, if I go back and read it, I'm impressed by it all these years later – it was really good stuff that others didn't appreciate at the time. There are many reasons why a paper can be rejected. It could really be because it isn't of a high standard, but it could also be because it went over the editor's and reviewers' heads, or because the reviewers are rivals, or because you're a newbie. One trend I found was that, the more papers I published, the easier it was to get more papers published – a lot of editors and reviewers will look up who the authors are, especially the first author. If the first author is "the new kid on the block", then the editor and reviewers will be very skeptical about the work. Of course, you do get better at writing papers the longer you've been doing them, but that's not the only factor that makes getting your papers accepted easier.

If your paper is outright accepted (the first option), then you don't really need to do much else – the typesetting people from the journal will often get in contact with you and ask certain questions about the formatting, maybe ask you for the figures in a different format, etc. There's nothing to worry about at this stage, they're just formatting, not judging your paper.

If your paper received the second or third option, and you decide to do the revision, then this involves two documents. The first document is your manuscript that you're revising. The second is a document that contains the reviewers' comments and your responses to those comments. What your responses are to these comments, and how you phrase these responses, will largely determine whether your paper progresses to the next phase or not. Doing the revision well will give you a great chance of either getting minor comments back, or getting your paper accepted. I won't go into the revision here, jump to the "How To Respond To Peer-Review Comments" section of the "Writing A Journal Paper" for more information about how to revise your manuscript.

Now, your journal articles are fantastic things – they're effectively validation from the scientific community that your work is of a high standard. The better the journal is, the better your work is seen. How do you know "how good a journal is"?

Dr. John Hockey

Knowing How Good A Journal Is

There's a whole world of journal articles – with the advent of the internet, the number of journals has exploded, but that doesn't mean that every journal is a good one. It doesn't mean that you should just submit your paper to any journal out there. Your supervisors know the journals – which ones are good, which ones are bad, and which ones should be avoided at all costs. This last category (the journals that should be avoided at all costs) is an interesting one, and I'll discuss this category first, as it's very important that you don't submit your papers to this type of journal.

There are journals out there called "predatory journals". Now, the term "predatory journal" is a little broad in Academia, and everyone has their own definition. Generally speaking, they're journals that aren't reputable. However, even that definition is a bit vague. Let me explain the different ways that a journal can be irreputable.

The worst "journals" (I put it in quotations because they're not really journals) are those that take your work and publish it under their own names. If you get an email from a journal asking you to submit a paper to them (especially if they address you by "Professor" or "Distinguished Professor" or something along those lines), then they're probably predatory.

Another subcategory of the "predatory journal" category are those journals that don't offer high-quality peer reviews. In some cases, a journal might send your paper out for "peer review", but those people who are reviewing it aren't qualified to do so. Other times, there might not even be a peer review process. In other words, these journals will typically accept anything. That doesn't mean that every paper published in those journals is of poor-quality – it means that there's been no "vetting" process, where the poor-quality papers have been eliminated. Sometimes, you find some really good papers in these journals, but other times, you find very poor papers.

A final subcategory of the "predatory journal" category is where a journal requires money in order to publish your paper. This is a gray area, as some people don't like the idea that you have to pay to get your work published. Others see the payment as weakening the journal's resolve to publish high-quality papers (they argue that the payment compromises the journal's integrity, as the journal will be more willing to accept a paper because they get money out of it). These are legitimate concerns, but there are not hard-and-fast rules about whether a journal is predatory because they charge you to publish.

If you want to find out if a journal is predatory, then you can look up that particular journal on Google, as others have probably posted something online about the "shifty" nature of that journal. Also, you can go to Google Scholar (scholar.google.com) and look up the journal. Google Scholar is a search engine for Academia. It's an incredibly powerful search engine, and in my opinion, the most thorough. Say, for example, you want to see what articles your supervisor has published. You go to Google Scholar and type in their name. Articles will pop-up that are attributed to them. So, if you think that a journal might be predatory, then you can go to Google Scholar and type in the journal name and see what articles they publish. See if any articles come from highly regarded Universities, or leaders in your field. If so, then the journal is probably fine.

Another very good way of determining if a particular journal is predatory is to use the following websites:

www.scimagojr.com

www.researchgate.com

www.journalindicators.com/indicators

www.scopus.com

All of these website are dedicated to ranking journals. The reputable journals are listed on these websites. So, if you go onto these websites and look up a journal and it doesn't show, then chances are that it's predatory.

Finally, you can go to Google and look up "predatory journals". Among other hits, you'll find lists from "Beall's" and "ResearchGate", which indicate their opinions about certain journals. If you find a journal listed on these lists, then chances are that they're predatory.

With the predatory journals aside, how to do determine how good a journal is?

There are a few metrics that you can use. Let's cover them.

Impact Factor:

The impact factor of a journal is the most common way of determining whether it's a good journal or not. It refers to the number of times the average journal article in a particular journal is cited.

There are many minor variations to this metric. Some quote the 3-year impact factor (the number of times the average journal article gets cited within the 3-year window after it was published), or the 5-year impact factor (similar to the 3-year impact factor, but for 5 years instead of 3 years). In addition, some quote the impact factor that excludes "self-citations"; self-citations are citations made by other articles in the same journal. In other words, this metric is designed to eliminate journals trying to artificially inflate their impact factor by strongly encouraging authors to cite other works in the journal (it happens all the time, and some journals won't accept your article if you don't cite a few of the other articles in the journal – they'll often use the excuse/reason that, if you can't cite other papers in the journal, then your paper probably isn't in the scope of the journal).

One thing to note is that, the impact factor, by itself, is not a useful metric – it becomes useful when you have two or more journals – then you use it to compare the journals. So, if you come across a journal that has an impact factor of 3 (which means that, the average article in this particular journal is cited 3 times within a given timeframe), then it doesn't really mean much. I mean, sure, it means that your article will get around 3 citations, on average, but you don't know how that compares to other journals. If, however, you come across another journal, and that journal has an impact factor of 5, then you can safely assume that this latter journal is generally more reputable than the former.

Dr. John Hockey

A lot of people struggle to figure out why "citations" are so important. I mean, what difference does it make?

Citations mean that others find your work pertinent to what they're doing. An article with many citations, like 10,000 for example, means that 10,000 other publications out there were "impacted" by that original article. It's a measure of how important an article is. The higher the number, the more important it is. In fact, academics have their own "impact factors", and if you compare two academics' metrics, you can get an idea as to who's research is more important (now, that assessment is not entirely accurate, as some academics don't publish much but still pull in a lot of grant money – grant money is a much better way of assessing how important an academic's research is).

A final word on journal citations; the number of citations an article can expect to receive is significantly influenced by the field it is in. Notoriously, articles that are published in "nature" or "biology" journals receive far more citations, on average, than papers published in "mathematics" or "physics". Over the last couple of decades, that has caused problems in Universities. Universities often rank their faculties and departments against each other. These rankings are very heavily influenced by the number of citations the faculties get. Those faculties that are aimed at those high-impact factor fields naturally get higher rankings, whereas those faculties that are aimed at those low-impact factor fields naturally get lower rankings. This caused a lot of problems – funding cuts, more pressure to perform, and less resources (to name a few). This imbalance in impact factors also affected the grant money coming from other places, like from industry and government; if you had two projects, one came from a group with some publications in high-impact factor fields, while another came from a group with some publications in low-impact factor fields, then the former group would have a huge advantage, as they would have more citations to their name.

To overcome the disparity among the impact factors of different fields, the "normalized impact factor" was developed. This metric is exactly what it sounds like; it normalizes the impact factor of a journal (and even articles) to its own field. If the journal was in a field that received far more citations that another field, then the normalized impact factor would usually bring it down and the two different fields could be more easily compared. This new type of impact factor is not that widely spread at the moment, but it is gaining traction. This metric is often shortened to the "SNIP", which stands for "Source Normalized Impact per Page". The SNIPs of most reputable journals can be found on this website:

https://www.journalindicators.com/

Time-To-Publication:

While the various impact factor metrics are a good indication of how good a journal is, the time it takes to get your paper published is also important – if there are two journals, one with a slightly higher impact factor, but it takes on average 12 months to publish a paper in it, then the other journal might be a better bet – you'll get feedback much quicker, you'll get published quicker, which will reduce the amount of time you need to spend doing your PhD, and your paper will start getting citations quicker.

While the time it takes to get your paper published isn't everything, it can be very helpful if you can get your paper published in 4 months instead of 12. Some journals are notoriously poor when it comes to the timeframe. I remember during my PhD, one high-impact factor journal in my field had a timeframe of around 5 months, whereas another high-impact factor journal had a timeframe of around 18 months! I wanted to finish my PhD while I was still young…not an old man.

The time it takes for a journal to publish papers is sometimes clearly visible on the journal's website – the journal might have it right next to the impact factor, or accessible on other linked pages. If the journal doesn't advertise the average publication timeframe, then you can usually get a good idea by looking at other papers published by the journal. Download 10 or 20, some on your topic, others slightly different, then open them up. Somewhere on the first page, usually around the abstract or in the footer, there will be two dates. One of those dates is when the paper was submitted to the journal. The second date is when the paper was accepted. Sometimes, there are other dates, like the dates of revisions – those are also useful pieces of information.

Acceptance Rate:

Generally speaking, the higher the impact factor of a journal, the harder it is to get your paper accepted.

In fact, the impact factor metrics lead to a "supply-and-demand" situation – most journals want to have high impact factors. The reason is because more academics will want to get their papers published in their journal. The journal can then select the best papers and reject the rest. These excellent papers will then get even more citations, which will further increase the journal's impact factor, and the virtuous cycle will continue. The problem for academics is that, as the impact factor climbs, the number of papers submitted increases, while the number of papers accepted for publication stays the same. As such, the acceptance rate reduces. On the face of it, it might seem like a good cycle – the problem is that, your paper could be rejected for any number of reasons. Sure, your paper could be rejected because it wasn't of high-enough quality, but it could also be rejected because the journal recently accepted 2 other papers on the same topic, so they don't want any more at the moment. Sometimes, the most mundane reasons are given, and unfortunately, it results in the paper's rejection. By a journal having a very high demand, they can be "ultra-picky" and papers that are very good could still be turned away because of minor issues. That's the nature of the beast.

Blind, Double-Blind:

There are two main types of peer-reviewing; blind and double-blind.

Blind peer-reviewing means that the author(s) of the paper doesn't know who the reviewers are. Double-blind peer reviewing means that the author(s) still doesn't know who the reviewers are, but the reviewers don't know who the author(s) is either.

Some fields contain journals that are almost all blind. Others contain only double-blind. And others are a mix of the two.

There are advantages and disadvantages of blind and double-blind review processes.

The major disadvantage that both types share is that, the reviewers often get more confidence by their anonymity. As a result, they are typically harsher, less understanding, and more "nit-picky". Over the years, I've had a wide range of responses from reviewers, anything from "This work is useless" to "The work will make an excellent addition to the field". It's just the way it is. Receiving harsh comments like the one I wrote shouldn't be taken to heart – it's often difficult for new students (and even old academics) to rise above that level of criticism, but understand that, the people reviewing your work are often your competitors. They're "fellow" researchers working in your field, it's in their best interest to keep you down. In some cases, they can't control their desire to lash out, and having the blanket of anonymity makes it all the more irresistible. I remember my first paper, I don't remember the exact wording of one of the comments, but it went something like this, "This paper reads like it's been written by a child" – it was that harsh, and it was my first paper. Other comments I received were along the lines of, "This paper doesn't add anything to the field", and "It is a long way from being acceptable". Well, fortunately for me, the editor didn't take those comments too seriously, and my paper got accepted. Now, it's one of my most highly cited paper, and it spawned two new niches in that field. The funny thing is that, I didn't change much on it after I got the reviewers' comments back.

Other times, reviewers will contradict themselves, or come up with a new list of changes for subsequent rounds of reviewing. If the reviewers had to stick their name to their comments, even if it were after the whole review process was done, then they would be far more reasonable. Alas, that's not the case, and I'm doing everything I can to try to spread the word about this idea to hopefully neutralize the problems of the blindness in this sense.

The major advantage that the double-blind process has over the blind process is that, theoretically, no bias for or against the author(s) will occur. In practice, this is not always the case. As I've covered before, your reviewer is often going to be a rival, and while they might have colleagues in the field, they'll likely be able to distinguish their writing styles from yours, so they'll know that you're not someone to be softer on. In addition, you can often glean the University from where the work comes purely by the innocuous details in the text, like the lab in which the research was carried out, or the references that were included (if there are a whole bunch from one research group, then there's a good chance that the paper came from that group). So, while the double-blind idea is good in theory, it often breaks down in practice.

LITERATURE REVIEW

We discussed publications, how they come about, what they're for, and which ones are reputable. It's now time for the literature review.

The literature review is incredibly important (it underpins your whole PhD), and is fascinating. You see, the idea of the literature review is so simple, yet, so many struggle to understand what it is. I was the same. There's one story of mine that highlights the frustration that literature reviews can cause:

I remember back in my Bachelor's degree – it was the final year, and we had a research project. For this research project, we could do it by ourselves, or in teams. I chose a team because I wanted a big research project – something that you could stand back at the end of the project and proudly say, "Yeah, we did that."

Anyway, while working in a team provided a lot of benefits, there was one time when me and another team member didn't see quite eye-to-eye. It was in the early stages of the project, and me and this other guy, Tim, were responsible for doing the "Literature Review". We had never really done one before – we had projects before, but they were rather superficial and reading a couple of articles was enough. This project was bigger, and we were expected to do a very thorough literature review. So, we went online and found all of the pertinent articles. We then divided them up for me to do half, and for him to do half. We went away for about a week, then we came back and each of us gave the other our half of the literature review (just as a side note, trying to split up a literature review is not a wise idea – ideally, the same person should write the entire literature review because they can then systematically detail the papers, but we didn't realize that at the time). He read my literature review, and he said, "This is crap!" I read his literature review, and echoed his sentiments. We both thought the other did a horrible job, and that our own efforts were far better. We argued about it for days, but finally we managed to come up with something that actually served as a literature review.

I didn't know it at the time, but years later, I looked back on that incident and realized the problems that we had with each other's half-literature review were the exact same problems that most people run into; my half-literature review had one of the problems, and his had the other. The two problems were:

1) I was *subjectively* reviewing the literature.
2) He wasn't even reviewing the literature.

99% of people who have trouble with their literature review have that trouble for one of the above two reasons.

To understand what a literature review is, we first need to understand what we wish to achieve by doing it.

At the end of the literature review, the goal is to identify gaps in the knowledge-base of a particular field. It's that simple. The reason why you need those gaps is because you need to formulate "the question" – the focus of your research. If there are no gaps, then what are you researching?

Now, at the start of the literature review, we don't have much. We don't know what has been done in the field, what trends and findings have been reported on in the past, and hence, we don't know what still needs to be done. So, what we have to do is get from "A" to "B"; "A" being not knowing anything about the field, and "B" being having a question to research.

To do so, **you do the "Literature Review", which means that you go through all of the publications on that topic, read them, digest the information in them, make notes about the method each paper used, the findings, any limitations, <u>then report on them and highlight the gaps</u>.** To draw an analogy to everyday life, it's kind of like being a movie reviewer; in order to review the movie, you have to see it first (i.e. read all the papers), then you have to give a review. Now, Tim "watched the movie", but when it came time to actually reviewing it, he didn't evaluate the work – he just listed what had been done and the findings, and then moved on. There was no talk about what findings were inconclusive, the weaknesses, or what was left to research. Me, on the other hand, I did do the evaluation part, and discussed what was left to research, but my problem was that I went a little too far and turned the evaluation into subjective criticism. Now, what I had to say about the problems of the previous works was right, but it didn't belong there – the idea of the literature review is to determine the gaps in the knowledge, and that doesn't require overt criticism, it doesn't require subjective reviewing. To illustrate my point, the following is a subjective review:

"Johnson & Johnson (1998) found that the bacteria had become immune to penicillin, however, their method was flawed and as such, their results were poor."

Now, the idea behind the sentence is fine, but the execution is poor.

The following is an objective review:

"Johnson & Johnson (1998) found that the bacteria had become immune to penicillin, however, their method was limited to a highly idealized environment such as…, hence, it remains unclear whether the conclusions drawn in that paper are conclusive or not."

The objective review expresses the same opinion as the subjective review, but the objective review firstly, describes how the study was limited, and secondly, doesn't incorporate emotional criticism. Now, anyone who reads that objective review will immediately know what Johnson & Johnson (1998) did, where it fell short, why it fell short, and as such, what a gap in the knowledge is. The research question is setup and all that remains is to overtly state it – but at this point, almost everyone can guess what it is going to be anyway; it will be something to do with the "conclusiveness" of the results – we'll be looking into the extent to which those results are valid under different conditions.

Doing a good literature review is key in developing a good question for a couple of reasons. The first is that, if you don't review all of the literature in your niche, then you run the risk of repeating research that's already been done. If you do that, then your research is no longer cutting edge, and that's what a PhD is all about. You don't want to get to the 5th year in your PhD (hopefully it doesn't go that long) and have someone say, "Yeah but, those other guys found that out 8 years ago already". You want to make sure that you're doing something original, and not unknowingly doing the same thing as someone else. The second reason why you need to do a good literature review is that, it helps define the field

– what's been done, what hasn't, and what should be done. It's key in being able to come up with a precise and pertinent question (note that, "precise" and "pertinent" are the operative words).

So, to do a thorough literature review, and setup your PhD, do the following steps:

1) Find all reputable publications related to your niche.
2) Read those publications.
3) While reading them, make notes that are pertinent to your field. Your notes should cover the following: what method they carried out, what kind of data they reported (variables, errorbars, types of graphs and figures), what findings were reported (trends, phenomena), how conclusive were those findings, what limitations were there, what future directions did they suggest.
4) Collate all of your notes and determine what gaps exist in the niche's knowledge-base.
5) Report your findings.

That's the crux of a literature review. Remember, a literature review is done so that, ultimately, a question to research can be formulated. It's imperative that a pertinent, focused, and original question is formulated for your PhD, and from the start of your PhD.

A final note about finding all of the reputable publications related to your niche. You can use resources like Google Scholar, where you type in keywords and find relevant articles. These resources are hugely helpful, but you can miss some publications purely by forgetting to search all relevant keywords. To minimize the chances of missing stores of articles on your niche, another good way to find publications is to go to the reference section of each of the papers you do have – check out who they're referencing, then look those papers up. Do the same with those papers, and so on, until you start going around in circles. Also, look all of those papers up on Google Scholar and see who's referencing those papers (under the paper, there'll be a label called "Cited By", click on that and you'll be taken to a page of all the papers that have cited this particular paper), then download the pertinent ones. That's an effective technique for accumulating all the relevant publications on your niche.

THE QUESTION

We already covered a little about "The Question" of a PhD, however, there's more to discuss.

Your PhD question is the most important part of your PhD. I know that a lot of people would argue that the most important part of your PhD is the research that you conduct. However, it's the question that makes that research important to begin with. If your research question is about Adderall-addicted teens and your data is about cats wearing diapers, then your data is kind of pointless; its only saving grace would be if you change your research question to suit the data that you have – and that's what happens 90% of the time. Unfortunately, what usually happens in a PhD is that, the PhD student goes through the initial stages of doing a literature review, formulating the question, then conducting a sizeable body of research, but after a year or two, the PhD question gets changed. It gets changed usually because there isn't enough research in the original question to justify a PhD. (There are other reasons why this change often occurs, but I won't go into it in this book – this book is about the academic elements of a PhD. The interested reader is directed to my other books if s/he is interested. This "switching" research questions can be readily avoided.) That's why developing an adequate question from the beginning of your PhD is so important; conducting a year or two of research then changing the focus of your PhD is, from a logistical and a project management point of view, alarming. There will almost always be part of your hard work that won't feature in the new direction – hard work that doesn't feature, doesn't contribute to your getting your PhD, which means that it was a waste of resources and makes your PhD harder to get – you have to do more work. So, it's far easier just to get your PhD question right from the beginning – it makes your time as a PhD student far more enjoyable, and it makes <u>all</u> of your effort payoff.

There are two general factors that dictate whether your PhD question is sufficient for your PhD. The first is whether it is "big" enough. The second is whether you have the resources required to answer it.

"BIG" ENOUGH

The first factor is always challenging for a PhD student to figure out on his/her own; if your department (or University) requires 3 journal papers submitted/accepted/published before you can graduate, then your question needs to be big enough to give those 3 papers. If you've never written a paper before, then it becomes hard to judge whether the results from a given research campaign will be enough for a paper (or 2 papers, or 3 papers, etc.). It's not that you can't predict how much data will come out of a research campaign (if you implement a certain method, then the amount of data coming out is almost a forgone conclusion), but it's more about how that data will translate into trends and phenomena – if you get 5 million data points, how many trends will that give you??

If you've never written a paper before, it's often difficult to go through in your head <u>before</u> you start conducting the research campaign and figure out what you'll get out of it. As you write a couple of papers, you'll get a good feel as to how many papers you'll be able to get out of one research campaign. And that's what your supervisors are there for – they've written papers before, so they should have a good feel. To give you an example of how quickly this "feel" develops, by my second year in my PhD, I could determine how many papers I'd get out of a research campaign before we even started figuring out the details of the methodology – I remember saying to my advisors, I'll get 4 out of this research campaign, and sure enough, 8 months later, there were 4 papers sitting on the desk. It might've been a fluke, but the same thing happened the next year, and again the year after that, and so on. Out of the research campaigns that I've conducted personally myself, and that my students have conducted, I haven't been off the mark, and there's been more projects than I can remember. I can even state how many journal papers there'll be and how many conference papers there'll be. So, your "feel" gets very strong, and it gets strong quickly. But to start off with, and even throughout your PhD, you should get your supervisors' input and ensure that you use their expertise – that's what they're there for.

RESOURCES

The second factor, the resources required to answer your question, is as important as the first factor. If you require twice as much lab-time as you've got scheduled, then that's going to be a problem. Likewise, if you need a certain machine, but you don't have it, or don't have the funds to get it, then that will also pose problems. Just like the first factor, it's quite demanding to have the necessary forethought to be able to determine what equipment you'll need, how much time you'll need, how much money, etc. However, your ability to accurately size up these needs develops with experience, and it also develops quite quickly. Fortunately, you have your supervisors there to figure out what resources you need and whether they're available.

Think of your PhD as like learning to drive with an instructor. You're the student learning, and your supervisors are the instructor. Now, when you hop into the driver's seat, you have control of the steering wheel and the pedals, but the instructor also has pedals on his/her side of the car, and intervenes with the brakes, gas, and steering wheel when appropriate. Under his/her instruction, and physical input sometimes, you learn to drive the car.

THESIS

Most importantly, the question you have for your PhD is of utmost importance for your thesis. I can't remember how many times I've heard stories about students get to the stage of writing their thesis and saying, "But I don't know what to write about!"… how about the answer to your question?? Going through 4, 5, 6, 7 years of research, then getting to the end and exclaiming that you don't know what your thesis is about shows a massive lack of clarity about what your PhD question is.

By precisely formulating the question, <u>and</u> adhering to it, your thesis is a foregone conclusion. You just need to go through the motions – it really isn't that hard – you've already put in the hard work, and the thesis is purely documentation of it. What's more, you've already written most of what needs to go in there (in the form of papers and general notes throughout your candidature), so it's just a matter of put it all together.

WRITING A JOURNAL PAPER

Earlier in the book, we went into what a journal paper was, what it means to have a published journal paper, and the stages of the publication process. This was important so that you could better understand a literature review.

It's now time to learn how to write a journal paper, as you'll undoubtedly need to write at least one during your PhD.

I remember during my PhD that, there were so many writing workshops, and even seminars designed such that you literally take your laptop there and just write. The reason why these workshops and seminars came about was because students were procrastinating with their paper writing. And the reason why they were procrastinating was because they typically didn't understand how to write a paper. I was in the same boat when I started. In fact, I remember going home and whining to my mom and dad that I didn't know how to write my first journal paper – it just eluded me. Unfortunately for me, those workshops and seminars didn't come around at my department until I was in my third year, long after I'd gone through the "teething" stage – that's life!

Nevertheless, I attended those workshops and seminars, and I found that my own process (the one I had developed out of necessity) on how to write a journal article was quite well-aligned with the process being taught. Since then, I've written many more papers, and done a lot of collaboration with other researchers, and guided my students in their paper writing (and done some of the paper writing myself), and the process is quite rigid and robust.

The hardest part about writing a paper is the start; "How do I start? Do I just start typing and hope that something good comes out? Do I start with the abstract, conclusion, introduction...?"

One of the hardest things for students to do is to silence that little voice in their head telling them that it has to be hard. Nothing even said that a journal paper must be difficult to write. In fact, the exact opposite is true. Just follow your instincts. Writing a paper is highly intuitive. All of those questions come from over-analyzing the situation, which comes from believing that it has to be hard. Trust me, it isn't. Let's go through it logically to show that there's nothing super-difficult about it.

To start writing a paper, you must first have something to write about, right? If you don't have anything to write about, then there's little point in writing anything. Following that logic dictates that you must have some data processed. Therefore, the first step to writing a paper is to process your data and analyze it. Find the trends. Determine the explanations for the phenomena that you found. You need to be crystal-clear about this information because it's the *foundation* of your paper. Without this data, the paper will crumble. So, you need to have all of your data ready, all of the trends highlighted and written out succinctly.

From here, you need to determine how these trends and phenomena work together. Which trends naturally group together to answer a particular question? Which ones don't? Once you've identified these groups, most of the hard work is done.

The next step is to figure out which trends (or groups of trends) to include in the paper – the general idea is that each paper focuses on one main idea, so if you have a few groups of trends that feed into different ideas, then you might want to split them up into separate papers. The problem that sometimes occurs here is that if you don't have enough data to split into more than one paper, you'll be stuck trying to make a paper out of a mish-mash of data. If you've done your planning carefully before the research campaign, then this is not usually an issue because you already know what type and amount of data you're going to get; the only time that this usually becomes an issue is when someone doesn't like publishing negative results. There's a bad stigma about negative results in Academia – most people think that if your results don't give something positive, then they're not worth looking at. People who think like that are not "all there", they're not looking at your work from a project management point of view. Let me tease this out more; when you have your own research going, you've pulled in grant money and you have a project to complete, would you be annoyed (or worse) if you found out *after* conducting the research (and having found out yourself that it gave negative results), that another group somewhere around the world had done the exact same research a few years earlier and didn't publish their negative results? I'm guessing you would. So, one of the major reasons why negative results are just as important as positive ones is that, it results in the scientific community using their resources more efficiently. Now, I know that some people will say, "Yes, but why would I give my competition help?" You can think of it that way if you wish, or you can think of it as: you getting more citations – if you publish your negative results, then that closes avenues to pursue when thinking about what to research. In other words, every literature review that is done on your niche will invariably touch upon your paper. That means more citations – they'll use your paper as justification not to investigate a certain question, as it will lead to a dead-end.

I always publish my negative results, and I've been a big believer in it since the very start of my research career. To my surprise, the papers with negative findings haven't suffered any loss in citations compared to my "positive" papers. In fact, in some cases, they've gotten more citations. I didn't understand why that was the case until I started digging through the papers that were citing my paper. What has ended up happening is that, my negative papers have created new niches in my field – many researchers have read my negative papers and wondered whether my findings will hold true under slightly different conditions. As a result, they've investigated it, and my negative papers have served as the backbones to their papers – as a result, I get more recognition. When I first started publishing these negative findings, I didn't expect them to have this effect, I just wanted to make sure that the data didn't go to waste (I wanted to salvage as much as I could), but it worked out far better than I ever could've expected.

When you've determined how to divvy up your results and trends, it's time to start writing the paper.

A lot of people like to start with the method, then progress to the results, then the discussion and conclusion, and leave the introduction for near the end (because you'll know what the paper is about after having done the other sections first). Those who use that approach shouldn't be writing the paper to begin with – if they don't know what they should be writing about to start with, then what's the point of starting already? Anything you write will be sloppy and ill-defined. That's where the process I wrote about above comes into play; by knowing what results you have, what trends you've found, what groups of trends you have, and what you want to say, you're in a much better place to start writing – you actually know what you want to write about! From here, it's not a matter of jumping around the place (from the method to the results, to the introduction, to here, then there, in a hap-hazardous way), it's purely a matter of going through methodically and writing the paper. You can now start with the introduction, then work your way through to the method, then the results, discussion, conclusion, and finally the abstract. It's a far more logical way, and your paper will be much more succinct because of it. Writing your paper in this fashion also helps train you to think logically about your work – understand what it's about, why you're doing it, etc. Developing that ability to truly understand what you're doing and why, will help you tremendously when it comes to writing your thesis.

Let's go through how to write each of the sections in your paper. We'll go in the logical fashion from introduction to conclusion, then the abstract.

INTRODUCTION

The introduction is probably the most enigmatic section in your paper – it is incredibly important to your work, yet no one wants to write it. I'm the same. It's often hard to sit yourself down and bring yourself to write the introduction. You've already done the hard work, got the results, and know what you want to write about, so going back to the introduction seems boring – it's kind of like watching a movie, then when you're three-quarters way through, your friend comes in and you have to start from the beginning again. Nevertheless, you should put effort into the introduction.

The introduction is the point where you take the reader's hand and guide them to your work. You need to determine who the reader could be; is it someone who intimately knows your field? Is it someone who doesn't know anything about your field? Etc. Your job with the introduction is to be able to explain to 99% of the people picking up your paper, what your paper will be about and why it's important. If you keep that thought in your mind while writing the introduction, then you can't go wrong.

For that to happen, you need to make the introduction like a "funnel". At the very start of your paper, you have people from all different areas coming to your paper. They all have different ideas and different amounts of knowledge about your niche. By the time they get to the end of your introduction, they should be able to explain what your niche is about, how it fits into the broader field, what question(s) you're addressing in the paper, and why it's important. That doesn't mean that you need to make them an expert in your niche, you don't need to explain all of the technical details; for example, if your paper is on Bio-Fuels, you don't need to explain all of the organic chemistry. Just explain, in words, what it's about. Take them by the hand at the start, introduce them to your field, then give them a mini crash-course in your field and lead them to your niche, the questions that exist in your niche and what your paper is focusing on. Note: don't put questions in there that you're not going to cover in the remainder of the paper. Only put the questions that are pertinent to your immediate paper. Save any other questions/gaps in the knowledge for other papers.

Now, in that last paragraph I wrote something that could raise questions with some people. I wrote that your introduction should cover why your research is important. Now, some people think it's appropriate to incorporate it into your introduction (and in your paper, in general), others disagree. The reason why some people disagree is because they see it as "sales-y", and not "scientific". At the end of the day, regardless of what job you have, salespersonship is an integral part. Even as an academic, you need to sell your projects, otherwise you won't get funding. I know a few academics who dislike "selling" their work, and they decided to "take the high road". That's all well and good, except that the "high road" doesn't only take you high, but it also leaves you "dry". If you want to thrive in Academia (and as a PhD student, you're in Academia), you have to sell your work. Having said that, if you don't include why your research is important, then it won't greatly impact the quality of your work, it'll just hinder how much attention people pay to it.

The introduction will invariably contain a literature review, perhaps not a very long one, but there should be one nonetheless – otherwise, how do we know how your research fits into the niche, and field? What's more, how do we know what questions there remain in the niche? The great thing about the literature review is that, the literature review you did at the start of your PhD will greatly help – most of the work is there already. It's simply a matter of pulling the relevant information out of that literature review, and including any relevant work since then. So, that literature review that you put so much effort into at the beginning comes in handy once again!

Once you've set up your field, your niche, the questions that your paper will answer, and why these questions are important, it's time to go onto the method.

METHOD

The method is probably the easiest part to write – you're essentially just listing what you did, and how it will answer the question(s) identified in the introduction. That means, what process you took during the experiments/simulations, what equipment, how long you did things for, what kind of data you got, what equations you used to process the data, and how you processed the data. If you planned the method well before you started your research, then there's little to worry about when it comes to its rigor.

As the method is essentially just recalling what you did, it's very helpful to take notes during your research about what you're doing, when, with which machines, for how long, how you're processing the data, etc. If you have those notes, then writing the method becomes even easier.

Due to the method's straightforwardness, there are only two points that I want to bring up. The first is that, almost every method benefits from including pictures and/or sketches. It's not so much the case that "a picture is worth a thousand words", but rather that, a picture can <u>succinctly</u> capture what the method is. Instead of having to read a bunch of words to glean what was going on, you can simply look at the picture and get the information much quicker, and in a less confusing manner (humans are very well adapted to visuals, so use them to your advantage). The drawback of pictures is that, they take <u>a lot</u> of time to draw well. You could easily spend 5 hours doing one picture. So, don't go crazy with the number of pictures you want to include, as that will take up all of your time – instead, focus on two or three key pictures. What's more, it's far easier to take pictures when you're doing your experiments – try to make them clear, with uncluttered fore- and backgrounds.

The second point I want to bring up about the method is error analysis. As I wrote above, some fields are very advanced when it comes to error analysis, while other fields are still stuck in the stone age. Some fields don't even talk about them – if you go to a conference and even whisper "error analysis", you'll might be escorted to the nearest door and asked to leave. Nevertheless, whichever type of field you might be in, a proper error analysis is always good practice. If you're in a field with a highly developed error analysis "culture", then your work will fit in (not including one will likely result in your work being shot down). If you're in a field where they don't even know the meaning of the term, then introducing it to your work will make you stand out as a leader in the field. I'm not going to go into how to do an error analysis here, as it is too complex for a "101" book – there are several very good books on error analysis, but even knowing the difference between "error" and "uncertainty", or "precision" and "accuracy", is a good start.

RESULTS

Dr. John Hockey

Structuring The Results Section

The results section of your paper can vary quite a lot. The results section "norm" (what should and shouldn't be included in it) can vary quite a bit from field to field. Some fields tend to keep the results section as a strict presentation and description of the actual results, while other fields also try to have a discussion about the results (discussion means: how the results fit into the bigger picture, the limitations, any trends that extend to other areas, etc.). The easiest way to figure out what kind of results section your paper should incorporate is to look at the papers in your field, and more importantly, the papers in the journal that you want to submit your paper to. If the majority of papers follow one type of format, then be sure to adopt that one. If there's a mix, and none of the authors have a preference, then the safest way to write your results section is so that it is most coherent and structured. Now, what does that mean?

There are usually a lot of data to present in a results section, and as such, it's often easy to get confused about the different sections – it's often easy to write an unorganized results section; you might present the data, then jump around trying to explain trends, and how they fit into the study, and so on. While it is natural to want to present some data then try to follow it through to the very end (explaining why it's important, etc.), if you have several groups of data in the results section, following this path becomes confusing (the reader is constantly trying to figure out where in the paper he/she is – what part of the niche, or what trend you're talking about now). The reason why it becomes so complicated, and often feels disorganized, is that, by putting the data, the trends, the implications of these data and trends, and how it all fits together, all in one section, you're bringing so many parts together. You pull information from everywhere and try to jam it all together – it's too much for people to handle – so many different thoughts in your head all at once!

So, while it is logical to present a group of data, then explain the trends, then discuss the implications and significance of these data and trends, if you do this for several groups of data, then the section becomes confusing and difficult to keep track of. If you have no option but to have a "results <u>and</u> discussion" section all bundled into one, then your hands are tied, and that's fine.

The far better way of approaching the results section is to present a group of data, explain the trends that occur, then move onto the next group of data. Do the same for that group of data, and then move on. Leave the discussion on what these trends mean, or the implications of the work, for the discussion – the discussion will be the next section.

How To Actually Write The Results Section

Once you've figured out the structure of your results section, all that's left is to actually write it!

As in the method section, a picture can be priceless. A well-designed picture, graph, or figure can portray more information, and more succinctly, than any sentence ever could. Think of any graph you've ever seen; chances are that you were able to get far more information from that graph in a few seconds than from a paragraph explaining the exact same results. That's the power of a good graph.

A picture, graph, or figure needs to do one thing; convey the information succinctly. In fact, I'm guilty of producing very simple and easy-to-understand graphs; I remember back during my PhD, one of advisors upon seeing one of my figures said to me, "This is not complicated enough. You need to have more information on it, more axes, more lines, put equations over it, and make it look so complex that you look smart. If the reader can't understand it, then that's their problem!" My other advisor was trying not to laugh because of how absurd that approach was; your figures are there to be understood, they're there to convey information, and to convey it quickly. The harder it is for people to understand, the less people will understand it. The less people understand your work, the less significant (or "impactful" it will be). In essence, it means that you'll get less citations and less notoriety. Don't be afraid to put "simple" figures in your work, as long as they succinctly convey the data you want to convey, then they're good.

If you make your graphs, figures, and pictures too complicated, then most people won't spend the time required to decode them. If you want to see how complexity affects "impactful-ness", then find a few papers with a high number of citations, then find a few papers with many complex equations peppered throughout the article. Chances are that, those highly cited papers don't flaunt this complex figure, or that complex equation – they state things so that most people can understand them quickly and easily. Those papers with page after page of equations usually have very few citations – I know because I have a few papers of my own that fall into that category, and I also have papers that fall into the former category (and those that present the data simply, do far better).

The only time when you should consider making a graph (or figure, or picture) more complex is when you have a lot of graphs in your paper – having 30 or 40 figures to paw through makes it difficult to keep track of everything, it also makes it hard to compare data. So, to reduce the number of graphs to a manageable number, making them a little more complex is a good idea – you trade-off between the simplicity of the graph and the overall simplicity of the paper.

As Albert Einstein said, "Everything should be made as simple as possible, but no simpler". It's a fantastic quote, and one to keep in mind while writing your results (and paper in general) – make it as simple as possible so that it is easily understood, but not so simple such that it becomes inaccurate.

Once you have your graphs, figures, and pictures, it's time to start writing your results around them. Figure out in what order you want to present each of the figures (the data and trends), then simply write about them. Explain the findings and the trends, but don't try to venture too much into how these data and trends fit into the paper's overall question(s) – leave that part for the discussion, if you can. It might seem mundane to mechanically go through and effectively regurgitate the figures, but what you're actually doing is pointing out certain features, and highlighting them. By doing so, you make them more important. For example, you could just present a graph of data, and it might be fairly obvious that a linear relationship exists between two different variables, but by explicitly writing about it, you call it to the forefront of the reader's attention – you're effectively saying to them, "Hey! This part's important, so remember it!" When it comes time for the discussion, it makes it far easier to reference a trend as you've already talked about it in the results section. What's more, the reader will be up-to-speed as it will be more prominent in their minds.

A final point to note is that, if there's a trend or group of data that raises immediate questions, then instead of trying to discuss these points, you can simply say that these questions (or points) will be covered in the "Discussion" section under "subsection…". It's completely fine to redirect the reader to another section for clarification, or even foreshadow that section. By doing this, you achieve two effects. The first is that you put the reader's mind at ease – they're not thinking, "But what about this?!", they know that you're getting to it in good time. The second effect is that you keep your paper structured and organized.

DISCUSSION

Now to the fabled "Discussion" section. We've talked so much about it, and delayed it until now. So, how do you write the discussion section? In order to answer that question, you need to first understand what the discussion is there for.

Your paper revolves around a particular aim (or aims) – those questions that your literature review pointed out all the way back in the introduction. That's the crux of your paper, it's the "raison d'être". That's where the discussion comes into play. You've got your results and found the trends, the next step is to talk about how these data and trends answer the questions, and how these items fit into your niche and field – what all of it means, in terms of the original aim and questions of the paper. That's what the discussion is about.

In your discussion, your job is to tell the reader how all of this research fits into your paper's aims, and the implications of your findings.

The discussion is probably the "most fun" part of the paper. It's where you can express your thoughts and opinions. You have a lot of "creative" freedom in that, you're not bound to simply describing a process or data, but rather interpreting the data and fitting it into the overall work. You can discuss what further avenues should be researched now, how conclusive the findings are, under what conditions things might be a little different (or that the results are conclusive for a broad range of circumstances), whether this research agrees with other research published, in what ways it differs and why.

CONCLUSION

In many ways the conclusion is a "foregone conclusion". Everything that needs to go in there has already been spelled out throughout the paper – the aim of your paper (its questions), the method, the results, and the discussion. The conclusion is just there to wrap everything up – it's a way to bring the reader back to the "big" picture of your paper and explain how your paper achieved its goals. During the introduction, the reader got up to speed with your field, niche, and the questions you aim to answer in the paper. From then on, their head was down in the details. It's time to bring them back up and remember the big picture.

As such, you need to briefly touch upon all of the sections you've written up to now. You need to explain what the focus of your paper is, the question(s) you sought to answer, and why they're important. Next, you need to briefly cover the general method you used. Then, you need to cover the major findings in the results (the "showstoppers"). Finally, you need to draw on the discussion section and briefly detail the answers to the original questions, potential limitations, and directions for the future. **You should highlight the most important findings, the real "showstoppers" that draws everyone's attention** – most people will read a paper's conclusion before deciding to read the entire paper – they want to see whether it's worth reading. So, by putting in the big findings, you entice them.

Dr. John Hockey

Once you've done that, then there's little more to write of the actual paper. All that's left are the abstract and the references.

ABSTRACT

The abstract is a 150-250 word paragraph that essentially sums up the conclusion, but even more – but with one twist. While in the abstract you go through the paper's questions, method used, some of the results, and the significance of those results, you don't incorporate any future directions (unless you really feel you must), nor do you incorporate weaknesses (that's just bad salespersonship) – you've already done that in the conclusion, so don't detract from the paper from the very start. Your abstract is there to grab people's attention, it's your first opportunity to convince the reader that they should read your paper. As such, harping on about possible weaknesses will drive people away – unless there's a major flaw with the paper, and in which case, perhaps the paper isn't worth writing – it might be better to repackage the material to address another aim, like "what not to do".

So, in the abstract, start with the aims of the study, then write a little about the method. Next, put in some of the results – you don't have to give exact numbers, or even trends (if you don't want to), but at the very least, you should detail what kind of results you have. Finally, you should explain how these results answered the questions of the paper.

It is customary to leave the abstract to the end, however, many people do so for the wrong reason; many people don't adequately plan their paper <u>before</u> writing it, so they need to figure out the "ins-and-outs" during the process. If they were to write an abstract before they wrote the paper, then they would struggle a lot, as they might not even know what their findings are or what the ramifications of them are. If you do plan your paper well before starting, then you could very easily write the abstract at the beginning, but we leave it to the end because it's essentially a concentrated version of the conclusion, and you can just work with that to make life a little easier.

REFERENCES

References are as useful as they are boring. The reference list is one of the most important parts of your paper. It's the place that justifies your literature review, and as such, it justifies your work. It's also the place that you draw upon to compare your work and findings to other works and findings. Without these references, anything said about other works could be false – who knows? We don't have the reference to back it up!

There's one caveat of a reference list that often goes unnoticed. The reference list gives your work context – it is essentially a representation of your niche. The more references you have, and the better quality those references are (like from high impact journals), the better your niche looks. The better your niche looks, the more important your work looks. Let me give you an example: I remember when I first started out in my PhD – I was reading papers upon papers. Many of them had 20 or 30 references, sometimes more. Then I came across this one paper, which only had 5 references. These references were also for quite general and mundane things. So, in other words, this paper was effectively in a niche of its own. While that increased my curiosity, it also rose questions about how valid the work in that paper was – if this is a new field, then there won't be many experts, and as such, the reviewing process might've been less thorough as a more developed field, purely because the expertise was lacking. So, purely by having more references included, a paper looks better as there's more backing it up, and it is being published in an established field. From this, the key takeaway is: include many references – 20 is a decent amount, and 30 is even better. However, don't go overboard, as it will increase the leg-work and not add as much – it will reach "the point of diminishing returns", so stick to around 20 or 30 references.

The number of names on a paper makes a big difference to notoriety. If you have only one name on the paper, e.g. Pete Johnson, then any time someone cites that paper in their paper, they'll cite the name and the year, e.g. Johnson (1998). That doesn't seem like a big deal until you start having more names on the paper; having two names on a paper is still fine, as both authors still get their names mentioned with every citation, e.g. Johnson and Smith (1998). However, problems arise when three or more names are on the paper; typically, all of the names that follow the first author's name get abbreviated to "*et al.*" (and it's italicized). "*et al.*" is a Latin abbreviation for "and others". So, if the paper has four names (Johnson, P., Smith, G., Kumar, I., and Wilson, R., 1998), the in-text citation will be: Johnson *et al.* (1998). In other words, only the first author gets the proper recognition and the others are grouped into *et al.* . It might not seem like a big deal, but it's often the difference between notoriety and lurking in the shadows. Of course, anyone who is interested in the paper will go to the references and see the other names, however, naturally, seeing one name popping up again and again will result in that paper being more strongly associated with that author than the others.

Another point to note about references is that, you should try to incorporate a referencing software in your work. Referencing software is a program where you enter your references and import them into whatever document you're writing. The beauty of this software is that, it saves you having to manually write out a reference for every publication you write. Instead, you enter it once in your referencing software and use it from then on. Another advantage of the software is that, each journal has their own preference for the referencing format, and you can usually change the format in the software with a simple click of the button. As a result, it saves you a lot of work trying to figure out where to put the names, how to abbreviate things, where to put the date of publication, or what font to use for the title, etc. All of this is taken care of by the software, and you simply import the reference in the right format, and where you want it in the document. One of the best, and most widely used, referencing softwares is EndNote. EndNote integrates with Word Documents. Zotero is another good software. The main advantage of this Zotero is that, it integrates with a wide range of applications, from Word Documents to LaTex. BibTex is another good, and very common, software for referencing – it is typically used with LaTex documents.

A final point to note about references is the "doi". The "doi" is an abbreviation for "digital object identifier". This is an alphanumerical code that indexes every article on the internet (at least it should, but some of the older papers still don't have these identifiers), so that there is a record of them – it prevents confusion and even plagiarism. In each of your references, you should strive to include the doi, as it is good practice, and often a requirement of a journal. If there are some papers that you can't find the doi for, then that's okay, as long as you got the ones that do exist.

AUTHOR ORDER

We touched upon the author order in the references section above, but there's more to discuss about it.

So, we know that the order of the authors makes a big difference to how they're cited. As a result, a paper is often attributed to one author more than the others (the first author instead of all authors). But, there's more. The order of the authors on the paper indicates to people how much each author contributed to the paper.

The first author is typically seen as the one who contributed the majority of the work (in other words, they did more work on the paper than any of the other authors). The last author is seen contributing the least amount of work to the paper. The authors in between are assigned credit in descending order, and limited by the first and last authors. In other words, if you have four authors, the first author gets the most credit, the second author gets the second-most credit, the third author gets the third-most credit, and the fourth author gets the least credit. That's the general rule in Academia.

There's one caveat to this rule-of-thumb. The last author is often seen as the highest-ranking individual on the paper. That's to say that, they're usually the boss. The reason why that's the case is that, most papers are written by PhD students. These papers usually feature the student's name first, then the supervisors' names. It has become a norm now, so that anytime you see the first name, you immediately think that it is probably a PhD student, and the last name is a supervisor. The names in the middle could be other students, or other supervisors. However, we are usually quite sure that there'll be a student and a supervisor in the list. Because of the working relationship (the student does most of the leg-work), the student is expected to come first. What's more, the supervisor often provides direction, but usually doesn't do that much on the paper – maybe a bit of writing, editing, but not to the extent of the PhD student (who does the experiments, data processing, etc.). As such, the supervisor's name should go behind the student's name. So, an Academic's preference for the position of their name on a paper often goes in this order: **first**, **last**, second, third,… They figure, "Well, I'm not first, so might as well be last so that everyone sees that I'm the supervisor and I'm in charge".

REVIEWING AND SUBMITTING THE PAPER

Your supervisors should be involved with the paper from the very start – they should, at the very least, stay up-to-date with what it's about and it's progress. They should also be giving you direction about the paper. Once you've written it, it's time to send it around to all of the authors. They need to read it. From there, they should give you feedback. That feedback could be anything from rewriting certain parts (hopefully not, and hopefully nothing more than that, as everyone should've been involved with the paper from the start), to giving you the green light to submit it.

If you get comments back, you should address them. Now, the word "addressing" is one of the sweetest words in Academia. To "address" a comment doesn't mean that you've done what it says, it merely says that you've considered it and responded to it in the way you think is fitting. Now, that response may be capitulating and incorporating everything, to rejecting it and giving a reason why. (Note that, the same goes for when you "address" reviewers' comments from journals.) Once you've addressed the comments, you should send the paper around for another review with your supervisors (unless you supervisors originally gave you permission to submit the paper once the comments were addressed). The reason why you need their permission to submit the paper is partly because they're your supervisors, but also because they're authors on the paper. Everyone who's an author needs to agree to submitting the paper <u>before</u> it's submitted – you're using their name, so they have a right. The same goes for you; if you're on a paper, then you have a right to see and be happy with the paper before it is sent off to a journal. It's one of the rights of being an author.

Some journals require that every author has "seen" the final version before you submit the article to them. If your supervisors have given you permission to submit the paper and you know that they haven't seen the final version, then it's best just to send it through to them and explain the situation. If they've given you permission, and they have access to the final version, but you're not sure if they've seen it, then it's also a good idea to check, just to make sure. They'll appreciate it – I know I do when my students make sure with me.

HOW TO RESPOND TO PEER-REVIEW COMMENTS

We talked about the peer-review process at length earlier in the book, but now it's a fitting time to talk about how to *respond* to reviewer comments.

You've put in the hard work, planned the research, done the research, processed the data, twisted it this-way and that-way to get the trends and answers out of it, and you've now written the paper. All that's left is to get it accepted for publication. To do that, you need to make it through the review process. A key component to making it through this stage is how you respond to the reviewers' comments. If you respond well, then your paper will get accepted. If you respond poorly, then the paper will get rejected (but you shouldn't take a rejection to heart – everyone, and I do mean <u>everyone</u>, has had a paper rejected at some point in their academic career). So, how do you respond to the reviewers' comments so that your paper will get accepted?

I've tried a lot of different approaches over the years. Those approaches have come at the instruction of other people, from my own mind, or from my students. Some of those ways were terrible, while others worked very well. I've taken bits-and-pieces from these different approaches to find the best combination. But, before we get into that combination, I want to cover some of the poorer approaches.

One of the worst approaches I've tried (which was at the direction of someone else, so I feel a little better about trying it out) was to incessantly deny the accuracy of a comment – it didn't matter if the comment was right, just deny it, regardless. That method, as you can probably imagine, doesn't win you too many friends – sometimes you can fool people into believing your point-of-view if you just say it enough times and with enough "gusto", but usually, you'll appear to be doing what you're really doing – just fighting to get it through without any consideration to accuracy. What's more, this method is not good for science – the idea of science is for the correct voice to win, not the loudest, and while there are some people out there who seem to win with their loud voice, inevitably, the day comes when their reputation crumbles. You don't want to be in that boat. I'm glad that I realized very quickly that, this approach was terrible.

Another poor approach is to respond to any probing comments by saying that it is a misunderstanding and the idea (or justification for whatever trend or phenomenon you're discussing) was expressed poorly. You then clarify to get around the probing comment without actually answering it. This method has one of the worst success rates.

Another poor approach is to cater to the reviewers' every whim. It will get you past some reviewers, but you'll inevitably meet a reviewer who just likes the idea of having someone listen to them without questioning. I've seen many instances where authors cater to every whim, only to be met with yet another round of comments (all new and fresh, and sometimes even contradicting the comments from the early rounds). What's more, you'll be hard-pressed to adequately address comments that attack the very foundation of your work. For example, one the most common comments that reviewers like to give back is: "Your work didn't include..." By giving this comment, it immediately makes your work look incomplete and inferior. Reviewers can say it about anything, all they need to do is identify what the next step of the work could be and cane the authors about not having done it. The funniest thing is that, it's an absurd comment, but it's a comment that can wreak havoc on your paper if you don't handle it in the right way. If you just cave to the reviewer's comment and agree that your work is incomplete, then that will really reduce the chances of your paper getting accepted.

Now that we've covered some of those incredibly poor approaches, it's time to get onto the best approach.

The best approach to dealing with reviewers' comments is to be reasonable. It might seem mundane, but the fact is that, many people can't be reasonable with their papers. Our papers are innately connected to us – we authored them, we put the work in. In essence, they represent us, our ideas, and our abilities. As such, the vast majority of people take any criticism against their paper personally, and it's understandable. Their reactions to these criticisms are usually in line with their reactions when someone takes a shot at the person themselves. Some people cower and agree, others retaliate with aggression. All of these reactions are wrong. They mean that you're emotionally involved with your paper. What's more, PhD students usually need papers to finish their PhDs, so any criticism levelled at their papers is also one more thing threatening their getting their PhDs – this heightens the emotional response. (Believe me, I've been there and I've felt those emotions, so I can wholly empathize.) These emotional reactions result in a loss of objectivity and reason. Let me explain what being reasonable, in the context of responding to reviewers' comments, is:

Your work isn't perfect, let me be the first one to tell you that. No one's work is perfect, especially not in science – not my work, not your work, no one's work. There is always better, and there is always worse. The only thing you need to worry about is whether your work is *good enough* to get published. It might sound strange for me to be advocating a "slacker's" attitude, but it's not actually a "slacker's" attitude. Everything that has ever been done in science (or any other form of Academia) is either good enough or not good enough – none of it has been perfect. Proof of this can be seen from many different angles. One angle is that, you have restrictions on funding and time. You can't spend $100,000,000 on one tiny part of one experiment. You can't have <u>zero</u> error. You can't have "no assumptions" in your work. Even mathematicians use assumptions, like axioms and other things that can't be proven. Their work is not perfect, it's just *good enough*. (I don't want to get into a whole philosophical debate here, but I'm sure that there will be some people who say that, an axiom isn't an assumption – we know that 1+1=2 is a self-evident truth. But, it is only true in your mind...what if your mind is wrong? You've made the assumption that your mind can accurately detect self-evident truths, hence, you've made an assumption.) The silver lining is that, these assumptions are *good enough* that everyone is okay with them. That's all you have to aspire your papers to be - *good enough*.

So, when a comment comes by that pokes a hole in your work, you need to acknowledge it, then explain why this hole is acceptable – perhaps, everyone in the field has the same "hole" in their work, or perhaps trying to patch that hole would require 3x the resources and time, which is impractical. Don't try to cover up problems, just explain why they're acceptable and how the work is still <u>valid</u> and <u>valuable</u>. By agreeing with the reviewer that there's a hole, you show to him/her (and the editor) that, you're being objective about your work – you're not trying to cover up anything, and you're open and honest – that's a rare quality from someone who's work is being attacked. It also shows you to be highly intelligent, as your arguments are correct.

Some of the comments you get from reviewers will be wrong. For those reviewer comments, you need to explain why they aren't right. Now, normally a reviewer won't like hearing that they're wrong (most people don't). But, if you juxtapose this approach with your ability to take fair criticism about your work constructively and objectively, then they'll feel that there's no personal attack coming from you; you're taking the "objective" ground, and you've proven it by magnanimously admitting your errors, so you're not interested in getting into a "war of egos".

By remaining objective, whether that's about your paper's flaws, or the flaws of the reviewers' comments, you come across as being far more trustworthy, knowledgeable, and rigorous than with any other approach. As such, your work looks better and it becomes *good enough*.

That's it for the journal paper writing, now on to the conference paper writing.

HOW TO WRITE A CONFERENCE PAPER

A conference paper is exactly what it sounds like; a paper for a conference. You usually write one of these when you present at a conference, however, not all conferences require papers. If they do offer that option (to write a paper along with your presentation), then it's always a good idea to do so. Conferences are about getting your name out there and mingling with others. If you only have a presentation, then once the conference is over, you won't make any more waves. On the other hand, if you have a paper to go along with your presentation, people who attended the conference can look over the conference papers today, tomorrow, even 6 months from now, and see your name there. It also helps when talking with people at the conference to be able to reference your paper in a discussion with them.

A conference paper is very similar to a journal paper; you have to have an abstract, an introduction with a literature review, method, results, discussion, conclusion, etc. But there are a few exceptions.

The first exception is that, a conference paper is not supposed to be as long as a journal paper. Where a journal paper might be 6,000 words, a conference paper might only be 2,000 words. A conference paper is not meant to be as extensive. A good way to approach a conference paper is to think of it as a chance to present one question and one answer to that question, only one. Don't have several groups of data, just focus on one, and do it well. The alternative is to focus on several, but focus on them superficially. That's not as good an approach as focusing on just one question/answer because you'll come across as "a jack of all trades, master of none". By focusing on one point, and doing it well, you show yourself to be an expert in that niche. People will be more impressed with your work than if you try to cover more questions and doing them less in-depth. As a side note, conferences often have prizes for the best presentation of the day, or the best poster, etc. The students who usually win those prizes (with political connections being equal) are the ones who focus deeply on one question in their paper and presentation.

The second way that a conference paper is different to a journal paper is that, the review process is usually not as stringent. For a journal paper, there's usually no time limit to when the paper needs to be accepted or rejected by. For a conference paper, there is. That fact alone has a massive effect on the quality of the reviews. Hosting a conference is a big deal – any University that gets to host a conference will be thrilled. However, what often happens is that it becomes a "all hands on deck" situation, where every academic and student is called to review papers and help out with the conference. As such, the quality of the reviewing process drops because the expertise isn't there. You might get a paper on a topic that no one in the University has adequate knowledge about, but because there's a deadline, and trying to get someone external to review it would take too long (or even cost money), someone at the University is forced to do it, so it's not that thorough. What's more, with so many papers coming in, the reviewers are pressed for time, and so they don't do a thorough job. That's not to say that every conference is the same, but many of them are like that. What's more, the conference organizers want people to come – it not only makes the conference look better (by having more presenters and attendees), but it also brings more money in the door. As such, their standards often drop a little to accommodate these desires. Furthermore, some conferences aren't even peer-reviewed, which means that there could be anything from a really high quality paper to a terrible paper – there's nothing preventing that from happening, and hopefully there will be some good papers going around. What's more, conference organizers often try to hold their conferences in some exotic location to gain greater attendance (a lot of academics and students want to go to Hawai'i for "work purposes"). As such, researchers will write something just so they can go – it might not be the highest quality.

A final way that conference papers differ to journal papers is that, many conference papers aren't available online – it's one of the ways that conference organizers entice people to attend the conference (if you want the latest research, then come along, otherwise you'll miss out). As such, writing a conference paper might not result in more citations, as very few people might have access to the papers. Those who went to the conference might cite your work, but you've got a limited audience. On the other hand, some conferences do their best to get your work out on the internet – one conference I went to published my paper on 9 different sites, so if you look up the paper there are 9 different ways to get it (those conference organizers were top-notch).

So, when you're writing a conference paper, just follow the steps to writing a journal paper, but condense them – make the literature review a little shorter, present less data, and focus on only one question and answer.

PREPARING AND GIVING A CONFERENCE PRESENTATION

Presenting at a conference can be a nerve-wrecking event. If you've never done one, then how do you go about it?

At this point in their lives, most PhD students have done some presentations before – they've made those slides and prepared their talks, and given them. I don't want to go too much into those aspects because you're probably up to speed with them. But just some pointers:

The first pointer is that, you should try to do one slide per minute of presentation time. Cramming too many slides into too short a timeframe results in confusion and the audience to forget each slide. Too few, and you might not be presenting enough information. So, one slide per minute is good.

The second pointer is that, you should try to make your slides "work for you". Your slides are there to enhance your presentation. If you could do your entire presentation without any of your slides, then the slides probably aren't worth too much. What you should aim for is that anyone who randomly picks up your slides could understand them without someone leaning over them and narrating. So, all the relevant information needs to contained in the opening slides so that the data slides don't have all this extra information peppering them.

The third pointer is that, your slides (and your talk) should be easy to understand; if you're on slide 7 and everyone is still trying to figure out slide 4, then you've lost them – they aren't paying attention to what you're saying or showing them anymore.

The fourth pointer is that, you should not use "cue cards", or read off a script. It looks unprofessional and people won't believe you as much. Contrasting that to someone who jumps up on stage and manages to pull out a 30 minute talk at will, using cue cards makes you look like you don't know what you're doing. In fact, I recommend that you don't practice your talk too much, either. You should memorize your slides, what order they come in, and what points you want to talk about for each of them, <u>but</u> don't over-practice your talk. Over-practicing your talk results in all of the spontaneity to wear off – your talk becomes robotic and boring.

The fifth pointer is to know your stuff! Know your field and know your work. Knowing your stuff is about more than the obvious reason of being adept at your field – it's about appearing confident. If you're confident, then that will ooze through your presentation and you'll make a greater impact. People can see confidence.

The final pointer is that, be prepared for question time. I've seen a lot of great presentations fall flat on their faces because of how the presenter handled (or rather, didn't handle) questions. I've also seen a lot of poor presentations get massive boosts through the presenters handling the questions very well. Question time is probably the most important part of your entire presentation. It separates those who genuinely know what they're talking about to those who managed to put together a presentation and pretend that they know what they're talking about. To be ready for question time, go through all the possible questions you can think of about your work and your field – come up with answers, and good ones (be up to date with your field). Also, gather people who know about your field and get them to ask questions – it's far better to get stumped by tough questions when practicing with co-workers than on stage – figure out what questions gave you trouble and plan good answers to them. Be prepared. Back in my earlier days, I would have a tendency to "read people's minds"; when I was in question time, I could figure out what someone's question was going to be within 4 or 5 words, and I would finish the question and answer it, all before the questioner had time to finish the question. Sometimes, I wouldn't even finish the question, and just give the answer right away – it provoked a lot of laughter from the audience. But it did something else as well – it made me look like I knew my field inside-out (it also came across as genuinely passionate about my work, which I was). As a result, more and more people wanted to ask me questions because they felt that they would get some really useful insights (and they did). Now, you might be wondering to yourself, "Why would I want to get more questions??" The reason why is because it's a good indication of how your presentation went. A presentation that gets 10 questions indicates that your presentation was fantastic. A presentation that gets none (and I've seen this happen quite a few times) indicates that the presentation wasn't worth anything – these things stick in people's minds. At a conference dinner or lunch, you might even get spill-over questions, which gets you're a lot of attention – you become an "up and comer" and "someone to watch". Conferences are all about notoriety – doing really well in question time guarantees you that notoriety. Put the prep-time into the questions and answers, and you'll reap the rewards.

TIME TO COMPLETION

One of the most important questions a student wonders to him/herself is, "How long until I finish my PhD?"

I remember what it was like being a PhD student, and yes, I remember asking myself that same question.

You can build up an estimate by seeing what work needs to be done, and then planning accordingly, however, sometimes factors come into play that the student wasn't counting on. As such, the time estimate that you come up with (which is derived from the work to be done), is not always that accurate. A far better way of determining how long your PhD will run for is by looking at how long previous students took to do their PhDs. That means, looking at the University averages (and spreads), the department averages, and most importantly, your supervisors' averages.

From these averages, you'll gain a much better insight into the timeframe you'll face. What's more, you'll get a much better idea of the completion rate for someone in your field at your University.

PERSONAL CITATIONS

We've talked about papers and journals and citations, but why are they important? Who really cares?

Those are good questions. Many academics will defend their citations to the death. The number of citations an academic has indicates how "good" they are, in essence. More accurately, it indicates how many times someone found their work useful. The greater the number of times, the more of an impact they have on science. Think of it like Instagram, or Twitter, and the number of followers you have. Citations to Academia (and academics) is like what followers is to Instagram. Some academics won't like me "degrading" citations like that, but, in essence, the parallels I drew between citations and followers is true.

Now, the more citations someone has, the more important they are, and hence the more funding they'll likely get, the greater chance of promotion they'll likely get, and the greater job security they'll likely have. All good things. What's more, it's an ego boost – like seeing your name onto of the leaderboard, for example.

While academics and journals share the idea of "citations", the precise metrics that are used differ. Remember when we discussed the different types of citation metrics for journals – 3-year, 5-year, normalized, etc. For academics, the metrics are a little different. Instead, we use two main ones: the number of citations, and the "H-index". There's a third, which is called the "I10-index", but it isn't as common.

The number of citations metric is self-explanatory: the number of citations an academic has over their lifetime (this can be broken down into years, or other timeframes). The H-index is a little more complicated.

The H-index is a measure of how many papers an academic has with a certain number of citations. For example, an academic with a H-index of 5 means that they have 5 papers with 5 or more citations. Likewise, a H-index of 20 (for example), means that the academic has 20 papers with 20 or more citations. Now, one caveat to the H-index is that, it doesn't matter how many papers the academic has overall. What's more, it doesn't even matter how many citations these other papers even have. All that matters is that, the number of papers the academic has with that number of citations. While the average H-index changes from field to field (remember that some fields are a little more lucrative with citations than other), generally, a H-index of 20 is very good.

One major limitation of the H-index is that it doesn't really tell you much about how many papers someone has. Sure, if you see a H-index of 10, you know that that person has at least 10 papers, but they could have 1,000 papers for all you know. Likewise, someone might only have a H-index of 10, but those 10 papers have 200 citations each (200 citations for a paper is outstanding), and this person just doesn't have any other papers.

One final metric that I'll cover regarding academic citations is the "i10-index". It's not that common, but it still floats around every now and then. The i10-index expressed how many articles with at least 10 citations an academic has. Again, you can see that a higher number is always better. For example, an i10-index of 20 means that this person has 20 articles that have at least 10 citations each. This number is better than 19 (which would mean 19 articles with at least 10 citations each).

If you want to keep track of your citations throughout your PhD, and during your career, then you should setup a "Google Scholar" account and a "ResearchGate" account. A Google Scholar account allows you to attribute all of your papers and citations to your name. As such, others can look your name up, find your profile, and know how many citations you have, and what papers you've written. A ResearchGate account is similar to a Google Scholar account, except it's more like a Facebook for academics; you add your papers to your profile, add what projects you're working on, your able to follow other people and they can follow you back, and every can see your work and the number of citations you're getting. Both of these social media accounts are fantastic for academics.

ZERO-SUM GAME

PhD projects are often viewed, and treated, as "Zero-Sum Games". That's to say that, they're often seen very rigidly. Some examples of how PhD projects are often treated as Zero-Sum Games are:

When you have team members with conflicting desires – one team member wants something out of the project, while another wants something else. These team members often view the PhD project as having limited funds and resources, so everyone can't get everything they want – there's only so much to go around. As a result, there are oftentimes when arguments and "fights" (fights in the sense of platonic fights) break out.

Another example is when a project changes direction during it course. People might think, "Well, we'll have a lot of data, so while it isn't in the same direction, there's still enough to collate and make a thesis – so, no harm done".

Both of those examples are the wrong way to look at PhD projects. PhD projects are <u>not</u> Zero-Sum Games. They don't have to be "either I win and you lose, or I lose and you win" situations, either. What's more, there's synergy in a PhD project.

For example, if you have two supervisors from different fields, they could work together to develop a good plan for the project (i.e. make it a multidisciplinary project). As a result, there's a synergy among the expertise, which makes the outcome greater than the sum of its parts. As a result, everyone could get what they want. Another example is that, by sticking to one direction during your PhD, you get better at it – every time you think about what needs to be done, every time you conduct a research campaign, you get more competent in that direction. As such, everything you do from then on is better – a synergy forms. As a result, the PhD project is not a Zero-Sum Game. It only becomes that if people start thinking that it is.

LEARNING ABOUT FRINGE AREAS

Your PhD is in a given field, and a particular niche, but that doesn't mean that you only need to know about that field. If you're doing psychology, then you need to understand statistics too. If you're doing chemistry, then you'll still benefit greatly by understanding project management fundamentals. If you're doing mathematics, then you'll still benefit greatly from understanding basics of risk management.

In fact, regardless of what field you're studying, there are many "fringe areas", and areas beyond, that you and your project would greatly benefit from knowing.

There are the obvious areas, like stats and report writing, that will benefit your PhD. But there are other areas, like project management and risk management that will greatly benefit your PhD as well – if you can think about how to structure your project, what possible problems might arise, and how to fix them, then when you get together with your supervisors, there'll be one more voice in the conversation, and better ideas will be formed. That can only help you.

Be open-minded when thinking about what "fringe areas" would be beneficial to your PhD. For example, most PhD students wouldn't even think that understanding body language would help them get them their PhDs – "I work with robots! Why on earth would I need to know about 'human body language' ?!" Well, if you zoom out of your project a little, then you'll realize that you'll probably be interacting with "humans" throughout your PhD – your supervisors, your grading/examination committee, other researchers, Bachelor's and Master's students, the list goes on. If you can figure out what someone's thinking without them even saying a word, then it gives you a huge advantage in determining whether your project is going well, what their thoughts are about your progress, if they think you're competent or not, etc. Let me ask you the following, in your defense, you'll be asked questions to which you'll have to respond. Don't you think it would be beneficial if you could read the questioner's opinion about an answer you just gave? I bet you'd agree with me when I say, "Yes! That would be awesome! I could figure out how I'm going throughout the defense, and if I gave an answer they didn't like, I could clarify before having my response set in stone".

Your knowledge about fringe areas makes a big difference to your PhD. In fact, I'd say that the only reason why I got my PhD was because of my extensive knowledge in those fringe areas (and it wasn't because I didn't know my field, on the contrary, I was nicknamed "Whiz kid" by those in my field).

ERGONOMICS

A final topic to talk briefly about is ergonomics. Ergonomics, in the sense of an office space, is the science of good body posture (more broadly, it's the science of efficient human use of his/her surroundings). The reason why "ergonomics" is important in your PhD is that, most PhD students don't know what it's like to have a "desk-job", where you sit down at your desk for 8 hours a day (or maybe more) and type away at a computer, day after day. Sure, a lot of students have come directly from a Bachelor's or Master's degree, but those degrees usually involve you being more active and not being stuck in the same position for hours at a time. A PhD is exactly that – there will be times (sometimes weeks or even months) where you'll be stuck at your computer writing away. For example, when you first start your PhD, you'll be doing a literature review. That will take many hours in front of your desk, finding articles, reading them, and making notes. I've seen it countless times, where the student first starts their PhD with a back as straight as Forrest Gump's, only to end up like Quasimodo.

So, make sure that you've got a good, ergonomic chair, even if it costs you a couple hundred dollars – it's a very good investment, as you'll be sitting quite a lot the next few years, and it's a small price to pay to avoid back, shoulder, and neck problems.

There are other ergonomic considerations, like where to have your monitor, mouse, height of the desk relative to the chair, etc. But those items are readily available on the internet. What's more, they usually revolve around your chair, which is a big factor.

FINAL WORDS

Committing to doing a PhD is serious business, and you should feel proud that you earnt the opportunity to do so. What's more, you should feel proud about every little achievement you earn throughout your PhD. At the same time, you should never lose sight of your goal. You should always remain hungry to finish.

Use the information presented in this book to help you succeed. In addition to this information, you need to remember two things:

1) Stay Positive
2) Continue To Want To Learn

If you stay positive and keep your desire to learn alive, then nothing can stop you – sometimes things won't go as planned, and you'll need to find solutions. Sometimes, things that you didn't even know could happen will happen. It's in those times where your positivity and your willingness to learn will get you over those obstacles. Remaining positive gives you energy, it keeps you motivated. Being willing to learn means that you direct that energy and motivation into learning what you need to in order to overcome those obstacles.

OTHER BOOKS BY THE AUTHOR

Do You Want Your PhD Now? The PhD Student's Stratagem

How To Get A PhD: How To Set Yourself Up For Success In The First 12 Months

Why Most Books on "How To Get Your PhD" Are Full Of S***!

The "John Hockey" Method For Coaching PhD students

Printed in Great Britain
by Amazon